Copyright

For more information, go to www.daviddenniston.com/physicians
For questions, e-mail: dave@daviddenniston.com
Or call 800-548-1820

About the Author

Dave Denniston, CFA is a financial advisor and author specializing working with physicians of all ages and enjoys particularly focusing on residents and fellows.

In working with clients for over 10 years, he has seen most every situation imaginable. His drive and passion to see every doctor's financial situation improve by eliminating their debt and reducing their tremendous tax burden.

His drive to help doctors came from the birth of his youngest child, Evangeline. She is his family's little miracle baby born in May 2012 four months prematurely at a weight of 12.5 oz (3.5 oz short of 1 pound!). As they were in the NICU for nearly five months, he had the opportunity to get to know many residents and fellows and listened to what they went through. He decided from then on that he was on a mission to help out any resident or fellow for free and the best way to do that was to write, speak, and meet with people individually to council with them on their financial situation.

He is an expert in a number of financial planning topics including debt reduction, 457 DCs, 403bs, and other retirement plans, asset allocation (where to invest), disability income insurance, life insurance, annuities, college planning, stock awards and options, and much more.

He has written other workbooks on a variety of subjects that are available for sale on Amazon.com including- *The Insurance Guide for Doctors* and *5 Steps to Get Out of Debt for Physicians.* He is planning to write other workbooks on other subjects related to physicians on investments, estate planning, and more.

He resides in Bloomington, MN with his wife of more than a decade, Cyrena, and his two children, Gabby and Evangeline.

For regular videos updates and newsletters on a variety of financial subjects, check out his website at www.daviddenniston.com/physicians or e-mail him at dave@daviddenniston.com

3

For more information, go to www.daviddenniston.com/physicians.
For questions, e-mail: dave@daviddenniston.com
Or call 800-548-1820

Summary

Today's world is an incredibly unfriendly tax & regulatory environment for physicians.

After all of the years of grinding hard work, being on call 24/7, and saving countless lives, you are likely getting paid a very handsome wage. And it has come at a cost.

Uncle Sam by cutting Medicare reimbursements (or at least discussing it every year) and by increasing your taxes due to the provisions of the Affordable Care Act, is out to get more!

However, the good news it that there are several steps that you can take to be proactive and keep more money in your pocket.

I don't pretend to have a magic wand and have your tax burden magically disappear in a puff of smoke, but there are several specific strategies that you can take to minimize your tax burden each and every year.

Explore and learn with me how you can minimize this tremendous burden and improve your specific situation. Take the next step- complete this workbook.

Learn how our tax system works and how it has changed over the last few years. Use this tool to reflect, strategize, and project yourself in the future. Revisit it on an annual basis.

If you would like any additional support and to learn more about how I can serve you, please feel free to contact me anytime at dave@daviddenniston.com or call me at (800) 548-1890.

Let's take this journey together and get you on the path to financial freedom.

Warm Regards,

Dave Denniston

4

For more information, go to www.daviddenniston.com/physician;
For questions, e-mail: dave@daviddenniston.cor
Or call 800-548-182

OVERVIEW	# Be Proactive! (and not with the pimple meds)

Young or old, high-earner or low-earner, what do we all hate? TAXES! We enjoy the things that taxes provide for us- roads, schools, libraries, retirement income, and security. Yet, we hate 'em. It's in our blood! It's why are forefathers dumped tea in the Boston Harbor. We don't like taxes.

Yet, there's a good way and a poor way to go about this process.

First of all, I have to confess that I am not a tax preparer nor am I a CPA. I am an independent financial advisor and wealth manager. Please remember that your tax situation is unique and you should run any of these ideas by your tax professional.

That being said, one of the things that frustrates me the most with tax professionals is how "inactive" they can be. They are great bean counters, but so many tax preparers don't help you figure out ways to better harvest the bean crop to allow you to keep more beans.

Often, investments and taxes are tied hand-in-hand. I talk with many clients about taxes every quarter. I've had the pleasure of working with some great pro-active CPAs who have unlocked the vast vaults of their knowledge to me in order to share this content with you. By utilizing some basic strategies, you can discover ways to keep more of your "beans".

Ultimately, I am doing this to help educate you and your family on how to find several ways to proactively reduce your taxes.

My job is all about helping you making smart choices about your money and I believe this workbook will be a standard to measure others against as you speak other financial advisors and tax preparers.

In this workbook, we are going to address the following:

➢ How the Tax System Works

For more information, go to www.daviddenniston.com/physicians.
For questions, e-mail: dave@daviddenniston.com
Or call 800-548-1820

- ➢ 5 Ways to Reduce Your Income (without getting a pay-cut)

- ➢ Managing Capital Gains and Dividends

- ➢ Be Charitable

- ➢ More Deductions & Write-Offs

- ➢ Back Door Roth IRAs

The exercises in this module are incredibly important in determining finding the right proactive tax planning strategies for you. For many of us, this can be difficult to look at. Sometimes, we need a guiding hand.

Don't hesitate to ask for help if you find you are procrastinating or just can't stand looking at the data on your own.

6

For more information, go to www.daviddenniston.com/physician
For questions, e-mail: dave@daviddenniston.co
Or call 800-548-182

MODULE One	How the Tax System Works

First, let's understand how our tax system works.

There are so many different kinds of taxes- income taxes, property taxes, sales taxes, business & occupation taxes, and much more.

For the purposes of this workbook, we will be focusing on three kinds of taxes- income taxes, payroll taxes, and capital gains taxes for individuals.

We aren't going to get into corporations, estates, or trusts because they open up a huge Pandora's box that will take up another two or three volumes of this book.

Anyhow, Income taxes can come from the federal government and from your state government. Some states don't have any income taxes (i.e. Washington, Texas), but most do.

Both the federal and state income tax systems are a tiered, bracketed system. This means the more money you make, the more percentage in taxes you pay. They can differ whether you are married, single, or married filing your taxes separately.

Also, the great news here is that this is the **EASIEST** kind of tax to be pro-active with. Most of our discussions will center on income taxes.

If you are familiar with tax credits or deductions or retirement plan contributions, all of these help to off-set income taxes at both the federal and the state levels.

We'll talk more about those later.

We'll take a gander at both the married filing jointly and single brackets because they are the most common situations.

Check out the federal income tax brackets below.

For more information, go to www.daviddenniston.com/physicians.
For questions, e-mail: dave@daviddenniston.com
Or call 800-548-1820

Single

Inc & ST Gains	Base Amt Tax	2014 Rates	Of amount over
0 - $9,075	0	10%	
$9,076 - $36,900	$907.50	15%	$9,075
$36,901 - $89,350	$5,081.26	25%	$36,900
$89,351 - $186,350	$18,193.75	28%	$89,350
$186,351 - $405,100	$45,353.75	32%	$186,350
$405,101- $406,750	$117,541.25	35%	$405,100
$406,751 and over	$118,118.75	39.6%	$406,750

Married Filing Jointly

Inc & ST Gains	Base Amt Tax	2014 Rates	Of amount over
0 - $18,150	0	10%	
$18,151 - $73,800	$1,815	15%	$18,150
$73,801 - $148,850	$10,162.50	25%	$73,800
$148,851 - $226,850	$28,925	28%	$148,850
$226,851 - $405,100	$50,765	32%	$226,850
$405,101- $457,600	$109,587.50	35%	$405,101
$457,601 and over	$127,962.50	39.6%	$457,600

For more information, go to www.daviddenniston.com/physician
For questions, e-mail: dave@daviddenniston.cor
Or call 800-548-182

Okay, now that you've seen the tables, hopefully your eyes haven't glazed over!

Let me break down an example for you to help understand this well. It's complicated, but easy to understand once you've grasped a hold of it.

I am going to look at the <u>married filing jointly table</u>.

IGNORING state income taxes, exemptions, deductions, or credits, let's say that you and your spouse are married. Together, you have an income of $17,000.

What is your tax? Looking at the table, they tax 10% up to $18,150. You are still in that income bracket. You would get taxed 10% or $1,700.

Okay, so let's say instead that you make $20,000. <u>You still only get taxed 10% up to $18,150. Then, you jump brackets from $18,151 all the way up to $73,800 with a 15% tax.</u>

Again, your tax bracket DOES NOT change for the first $18,150. However, it does change for the additional amount above it. In the case of $20,000, you would get taxed $1,815 for the first $18,150 in income PLUS 15% on $1,850 or $277.50 for a <u>grand total of $2,092.50</u>.

Your income is currently in the 15% bracket, BUT your effective tax rate is <u>10.46%.</u>

If instead, you made $73,800, your income is STILL in the 15% bracket, BUT in this case your taxes paid is <u>$10,162.50</u> leading to an effective tax rate of <u>13.8%.</u>

See how as your income increases while staying in your tax bracket, your effective tax rate can move up?

Also, you want to be very aware of when you may move from one tax bracket to another.

There is a tremendous jump for married filing jointly from $73,800 to $73,801, **from 15% to 25%**. That's a 10% jump! That means your effective taxes will grow exponentially (if you are married) for every dollar above $73,800.

If at all possible, you would rather stay in the 15% bracket! But there is more to consider...

<u>I would be remiss in this section if I didn't briefly discuss tax credits and tax deductions.</u>

Tax credits are the BEST possible kind of friendly, tax favorable treatment one can have. Essentially, you are getting a dollar back for every dollar they credit you. You could possibly get money back on a return where you had no income and didn't pay into the tax system, by getting tax credits. I saw this happen with the homebuyer's act in 2009 where a client got money from the government even though they never paid taxes (due to tax write-offs in the previous year).

There are also tax deductions and exemptions that offset the income that you generate.

For more information, go to www.daviddenniston.com/physicians.
For questions, e-mail: dave@daviddenniston.com
Or call 800-548-1820

The most famous of these is the choice between ITEMIZING your taxes (i.e. using the available deductions) or using the minimum STANDARD DEDUCTION.

The standard deduction in 2014 is $6,200 if you are single, $12,400 if you are married.

Think about this for a minute- this means that if you are married- at a minimum, the first $12,400 that you make WILL NOT have a federal income tax because it offsets dollar for dollar the first $12,400 of your income.

Essentially, if you are making $18,150, you are ONLY getting federal income tax on $5,750 for a grand total of $575. *There is one provision to be aware of here: the standard deduction starts to phase out at $305,050 if you are married filing jointly or $254,200 if you are single.* If possible, you want to maintain that deduction!

Instead, think of the tax brackets like this, adjusted for the standard deduction (for married filing jointly) in REALITY:

Dave's Adjusted Married Filing Jointly

Inc & ST Gains	Base Amt Tax	2014 Rates	Of amount over
0 - $12,400	0	0%	
$12,401 - $30,551	0	10%	
$30,552 - $86,200	$1,815	15%	$30,551
$86,201 - $161,250	$10,162.50	25%	$86,200
$161,251 - $239,250	$28,925	28%	$161,250

For more information, go to www.daviddenniston.com/physician
For questions, e-mail: dave@daviddenniston.com
Or call 800-548-182

Alright, we've spent quite a bit of time on income taxes. Let's also take some time to understand capital gains taxes.

Capital gains are the taxes that one pays on investments after they have been sold (assuming that there is a gain). This can occur in real estate, stocks, bonds, small businesses, and much more!

There are two different types of capital gains taxes- long term and short term. Short-term capital gains are incurred when you bought and sold an asset within a year. Whereas long-term capital gains occur when you have held an asset longer than a year.

Short-term gains are taxed at ORDINARY INCOME rates from the previously mentioned tables whereas long-term gains are taxed at SPECIAL lower rates.

Thus, you want as much as possible to utilize long term capital gains, you want to hold your appreciated assets *for at least one year*.

Why does the government care?

The government is incentivizing investors to make long-term investments. They want people to put money into start-up companies and venture capital as well as to reduce the volatility of the financial markets.

Let's take a look at the table for capital gains rates.

LT Capital Gains- Joint (Single)	2014 Rates
0 - $73,800 (0 - $36,900)	0%
$73,801 - $457,600 ($36,901 - $405,100)	15%
$457,601 and over ($405,101 and over)	20%

For more information, go to www.daviddenniston.com/physicians.
For questions, e-mail: dave@daviddenniston.com
Or call 800-548-1820

This is similar to the income brackets, but compressed. Do you see how investors could possibly have ZERO tax on capital gains if they are in the lower brackets?

That's awesome!

Consider the implications of this… if you are a resident or fellow and you have inherited stock that is wayyy higher than the cost basis. The BEST TIME to sell it from a tax perspective is WHILE you are a resident or a fellow. You may pay NO TAXES on the capital gain when you consider the standard deduction gives you a free pass on the first $12,400 of your income.

Alternatively, if you are making more than $450,000, capital gain taxes will **be far more favorable** than ordinary income. At that stage, ordinary income is at the **39.6% bracket**!

With long-term capital gains at 20%, that is nearly half of your normal income tax bracket!

Let's take a moment to also understand how the Affordable Care Act (i.e. Obamacare) has effected investment income.

Besides pushing up the top income tax bracket from 35% to 39.6%, the ACA ALSO added an additional tax on investment income.

A provision within the law adds a 3.8% tax on the LESSER of net investment income OR excess of modified adjusted gross income (AGI) over $250,000 if you are married or $200,000 if you are single.

This means that for someone making over $250,000, that your capital gains rate is actually 23.8% NOT 20%.

While, it is still lower than your income tax rate, this should give us extra pause before selling positions with capital gains once you are making more dough.

Again, another reason to sell appreciated positions while you are in residency or fellowship!

Keep in mind that for the most part, capital gain taxes are within your control! You can decide when you want to sell appreciated (or depreciated) positions. You can be pro-active and look in a given tax year to see how close you may be to bumping against a tax bracket, and then decide whether or not to harvest those gains.

It is in your control!

Finally, let's discuss payroll taxes.

They are the social program taxes that support the entitlement programs of social security, medicare, and Medicaid.

Without a doubt, payroll taxes are the HARDEST tax to avoid. There are NO standard deductions or itemized deductions or credits that can off-set payroll taxes.

For more information, go to www.daviddenniston.com/physician
For questions, e-mail: dave@daviddenniston.com
Or call 800-548-182

They are pretty much out of your control unless you own a clinic in a small partnership or as a sole proprietor.

What is completely different about payroll taxes is that they are paid by <u>BOTH</u> the employer and the employee. <u>Also, they are only exercised on EARNED INCOME</u>. This means that if you are not working or are retired, you are NOT paying pay-roll taxes.

If you are self-employed, you cannot avoid the responsibility. There too, you also pay as BOTH the employer and the employee.

If you are an employee, the employer will withhold all of these taxes and send in a check to the IRS

The Affordable Care Act (Obamacare) also comes into play here too. Once you are making over a certain dollar amount, you pay an ADDITIONAL medicare tax. However, most employers ARE not sending this in on your behalf.

Many doctors got caught off-guard in 2013 when they found out they had to pay more taxes than normal due to the ADDITIONAL medicare tax.

Check out the table below for more details.

Payroll Taxes	2014 Rates
0 - $117,000 Social Security	6.2% Employer
0 - $117,000 Social Security	6.2% Employee
0 – Unlimited Medicare	1.45% Employer
0 – Unlimited Medicare	1.45% Employee
$250,000 (JT) and > Medicare (NEW) $200,000 (sngle)) & > (NEW)	0.9% Employee
TOTAL EMPLOYEE < 250k	7.65% SUB-TOTAL
TOTAL EE and ER < 250k (jt), 200k (sgle)	**15.30% TOTAL**
TOTAL EE and ER > 250K (jt), 200k (sgle)	**16.20% TOTAL**

Let's understand a few things about this table:

For more information, go to www.daviddenniston.com/physicians.
For questions, e-mail: dave@daviddenniston.com
Or call 800-548-1820

> ➢ Social Security Taxes are currently CAPPED at $117,000 and will rise with social security benefits on an annual basis. *In future budget negotiations between Congress & the President, I imagine this could be a major discussion point. Imagine how your taxes may go up, if there is NO cap on social security taxes.*

> ➢ Medicare taxes have NO CAP. You pay Medicare taxes no matter how high your earned income is.

> ➢ The Affordable care act increased Medicare taxes by almost 1% if you are making over $250k jointly or $200k as a single taxpayer. Again, your EMPLOYER is likely NOT withholding this tax. You may need to adjust your withholding to make up for the difference to avoid owing taxes in future years.

Okay, now let's tie this altogether!

Let's look at a couple of scenarios taking ONLY in consideration the standard deduction and no other exemptions, deductions, or credits (this isn't entirely realistic, but gives you a very good snapshot of how taxes can work).

Dr. Jones, a married primary care physician employed by a hospital is earning **$200,000. He has no investments…**

First, let's calculate his **income tax**. Dr. Jones and his wife have a standard deduction of $12,400. This means his federal taxable income is only $187,600.

He is currently in the *28% bracket*, with income between $148,851 to $226,850.

However, his federal income effective tax rate is **lower**. He pays $28,925 (the previous taxes from below the 28% bracket) + $10,849.72 (the tax above $148,851) for a total of $39,774.72 or an *effective tax of 19.9%* on the $200,000 income.

Dr. Jones is working and his employer also withholds and pays **payroll** taxes right out of his paycheck.

He will pay 6.2% Social Security Taxes on the first $117,000 for a total of $7,020. His employer will also pay that amount to the government, but it doesn't come out of Dr. Jones' pocket.

Then, he will pay 1.45% Medicare taxes on ALL of his earned income, $200,000 for a total of $2,900.

Let's add this all up. **This is a grand total of taxes of $49,694.72 on income of $200,000 or total taxes paid of 24.8%.**

Let's see how this compares to Dr. Smith.

Dr. Smith, a married orthopaedic surgeon, owns his own solo practice with various support staff and is earning **$500,000. He had a very good year in his investments, and had realized long-term capital gains of $20,000.**

For more information, go to www.daviddenniston.com/physician
For questions, e-mail: dave@daviddenniston.com
Or call 800-548-182

First, let's calculate his **income tax**. Dr. Smith and his wife DO NOT have a standard deduction because their income is well above $305,040. This means his <u>federal taxable income is STILL $500,000</u>.

He is currently in the *39.6% bracket*, with income ABOVE $457,600.

However, his federal income effective tax rate is **lower**. He pays $127,962.50 (the previous taxes from below the 35% bracket) + $16,790.40 (the tax above $457,600) for <u>a total of $144,752.90</u> or an *effective tax of 28.95%* on the $500,000 income.

Dr. Smith is working and his employer also withholds and pays **payroll** taxes right out of his paycheck.

He will pay 6.2% <u>Social Security Taxes</u> on the first $117,000 for <u>a total of $7,020</u>. His employer will also pay that amount to the government, but it doesn't come out of Dr. Smith's pocket.

Then, he will pay 1.45% <u>Medicare taxes</u> on ALL of his earned income- $500,000, PLUS 0.9% on all income over $250,000 (joint) due to Obamacare for a <u>total of $9,500</u>.

Lastly, let's not forget that he had investment income- **capital gains** of $20,000. Let's assume that his capital gains/other investment income were lower than his MAGI. Because his income is over $250,000 and he is in the 39.6%, he will owe 20% capital gains PLUS 3.8% due to the affordable care act for a total of 23.8% on the $20,000 capital gains or $4,760.

Let's add this all up. **This is a grand total of taxes of $166,033 on income of $520,000 (includes the capital gains) or total taxes paid of 31.9%.** Now, you understand the basics! I have some homework and action steps to help you gain more insight into your specific situation.

1.1 Action Step: Get the last copy of your paystub. Gather together information on your tax situation and fill in the information below. <u>This will be very important to refer to later!</u>:

Current Compensation Year-to-Date:_____

Annualized Compensation :_____

(HINT: take current compensation and multiple by 12 divided by the # of months compensated already. For example, using an end of the month May check, multiply amount x 12/5)

Current Social Security Tax Year-to-Date:_____

Annualized Social Security Tax (max of $7,020 in 2014):_____

Current Medicare Tax Year-to-Date:_____

For more information, go to www.daviddenniston.com/physicians.
For questions, e-mail: dave@daviddenniston.com
Or call 800-548-1820

Annualized Medicare Tax (NO max in 2014):_____

Current State Income Tax Year-to-Date:_____

Annualized State Income Tax :_____

Current Federal Income Tax Year-to-Date:_____

Annualized Federal Income Tax :_____

Estimated Year-End Bonus:_____

1.2 **Action Step:** Get the last copy of your tax return. Gather information from the first two pages of form 1040, Schedule A, and Schedule D. <u>This will be very important to refer to later!</u> (Note the line items are from the 2013 tax return):

Line 7- Wages, Salaries, etc:_____   **Line 9a- Ordinary Dividends**_____

Line 8a- Taxable Interest:_____

Line 13- Capital Gains(Losses)_____

   Schedule D- Part I- ST Gains- Line 7_____

   Schedule D- Part 2- Losses Forward- Line 13_____

   Schedule D- Part 2- LT Gains- Line 15_____

Line 37- Adjusted Gross Income (AGI):_____

Line 40- Itemized Deductions:_____

   Schedule A- Line 5a- State Income Tax_____

Line 42- Exemptions: _____

Line 43- Taxable Income:_____

Line 57- Unreported ss & medicare tax:_____

Line 61- Total tax:_____

Line 72- Total payments:_____

For more information, go to www.daviddenniston.com/physician
For questions, e-mail: dave@daviddenniston.cor
Or call 800-548-182

1.3 Action Step: Review over the data that you listed above. How does your wages compare to your AGI? How does your AGI compare to your taxable income? Are you itemizing or taking the standard deduction? How much do you have in exemptions? Note that SOCIAL SECURITY TAXES are not usually included here.

What have your learned about your tax situation?

Write your thoughts down below.

_____

_____

_____

_____

_____

1.4 Action Step: Focus on the last two lines above- Line 61 TOTAL TAX & Line 72 TOTAL PAYMENTS. Were you paying ENOUGH to the government or instead were you paying TOO MUCH? Going extreme one way or the other could lead to consequences.

I personally feel that a refund of $1,000 to $2,000 is reasonable. This gives you some cushion How much of a refund are you getting (or payment are you making)?

If you were getting a LARGE refund ($5,000 and above), you are withholding TOO MUCH. You are essentially LOANING money to Uncle Sam for FREE. I am all for being patriotic, but I won't lend much money to our irresponsible government. I know, it feels good to get a big "paycheck" when you get your refund. But instead, couldn't you increase your monthly cash flow?

Then you could pay down your debts quicker. Or perhaps invest more on a monthly basis.

In order to correct this issue, INCREASE the number of exemptions on your pay-stub at work.

Conversely, if you are writing out big checks to Uncle Sam every April, consider DECREASING the number of exemption so that they withhold MORE taxes. Writing big checks is painful for many of us!

Write down your thoughts below.

_____

For more information, go to www.daviddenniston.com/physicians.
For questions, e-mail: dave@daviddenniston.com
Or call 800-548-1820

_____

_____

MODULE	
Two	# 5 Ways To Reduce Your Income (Without Taking a Paycut)

Now that we've covered the basics of taxes and how they work, let's explore several easy ways to reduce income taxes.

1) Paycheck- Contribute to 401k or 403b

I have one basic rule, a mere three words, that I have spoken about in seminars at the Mayo Clinic and with the Minnesota Medical Association time and time again. Pay close attention…

PAY YOURSELF FIRST.

Let's emphasize this again, everybody now repeat after me…

PAY YOURSELF FIRST.

For more information, go to www.daviddenniston.com/physician
For questions, e-mail: dave@daviddenniston.co
Or call 800-548-182

This mantra is simple. Yet for many of us, it can be very hard to apply.

First, just simply- get started! **Contribute to your 401k (or 403b for non-profits i.e. many hospitals). It not only counts towards retirement, but it lowers your income taxes.**

This money comes right out of your paycheck, withheld by your employer- it never even sees your tax return! This is because the income reported on your tax return is ADJUSTED by these kinds of tax deductions.

Think about this for a second. By contributing to your 401k, every dollar you put in gives you a discount on your federal income taxes (but not FICA taxes). For example, if you are in the 25% bracket, and you contribute $10,000- you have just lowered your taxes by $2,500! That's like a 25% rate of return on your money TODAY that can grow tax-free until you take it out someday, when it will be taxed likely at a lower bracket.

Of course, many of us are actually paying WAY more than 25%- including state income taxes- often 40% to 50%! That's an even higher discount on your money.

Secondly, at a minimum, **make sure to contribute at least up to the maximum match that your employer provides.** If your employer matches dollar for dollar, this is like an automatic 100% return. Even if your employer matches 50 cents or 25 cents on the dollar, that is still like a 50% or 25% return just for contributing.

Altogether, with a match, you may have just doubled your money by being tax efficient!

Lastly, **get close to maxing out your maximum contribution in order to lower both your federal and state income taxes.** If you are under 50 years old, the maximum you can put in the 401k is $17,500 in 2014. If you are over 50 years, you can do an additional catch-up contribution of $5,500 for a total of $23,000!

2) Paycheck- Contribute to 401k PLUS 457 DC or 403b PLUS 457 DC

Here's a HUGE point that many doctors miss out on. Especially if you work for a hospital- you are likely to have MORE than one retirement plan.

You are very likely to have TWO (or more) retirement plans.

See the IRS has a few weird quirks in the tax system. You can check out more information here.

For more information, go to www.daviddenniston.com/physicians.
For questions, e-mail: dave@daviddenniston.com
Or call 800-548-1820

Essentially, it boils down to this- you CANNOT contribute the max to both a 401k AND a 403b (or SIMPLE IRA, SEP IRA, etc). The most you can put between the two plans is the usual $17,500 plus catch-up provisions.

However, you CAN contribute $17,500 plus ANOTHER $17,500 to a 401k (or 403b) AND a 457(b).

This is because 457(b) are subject to completely different provisions under a separate part of the IRS code. Note that most employers DO NOT match in the 457(b). So, you are better off taking advantage of the 401k or 403b first.

However, as you have your debts paid off and your discretionary income skyrockets, take advantage of this provision!

If you are paying 50% between federal and state income taxes- this means you could easily be saving $17,500 in taxes by maxxing out both plans!!! Every year!!

Remember, PAY YOURSELF FIRST!

3) Paycheck & line 25 of the 1040- Contribute to HSA

Yet another awesome way to take advantage of the paycheck, pre-tax return deductions is to also fund money into an HSA (health savings account).

Contribution limits are significantly less than 401k/403b/457(b) limits- $3,300 for individuals or $6,550 for families plus a $1,000 catch-up limit.

However, this converts an expense using money that has already been taxed to instead be an expense using pre-tax dollars. Additionally, when you take the money out for health specific reasons and expenses- it comes out TAX FREE.

This means that you could save and save (if you aren't currently having any health issues) and have money stocked for medical expenses that will come OUT TAX-FREE as well as having been tax-deduction when you put in the money.

Definitely, max this out!

You can see this line on both your paycheck and possibly line 25 of the 1040 if you self-funded an HSA.

4) Line 12 of the 1040- Set-up business or moonlight as a consultant

The American tax code is set up to benefit one person- the business owner.

For more information, go to www.daviddenniston.com/physician
For questions, e-mail: dave@daviddenniston.co
Or call 800-548-182

If you want to take advantage of the tax system and work its loopholes (legally), check out line 12 of the 1040 and Schedule C. There are many many expenses that business owners can take advantage of.

I know that all of us are so busy and you may not have a single extra second to dedicate towards another money-making venture.

However, I strongly encourage you to start your own small business. Many people today sell trinkets or hobbies through E-Bay or Amazon.com. One of my friends who worked for a Fortune 500 company as an analyst, yet found the time to "moonlight" to sell mixed martial arts equipment on Amazon.com. He is now making more money from the part-time business than from his full-time job and recently left his full-time job to go after the "part-time" gig.

What are your talents? What are your passions? What is something that wouldn't take a whole lot of time and have a low barrier to starting up?

NOTE: The IRS has some very specific guidelines regarding losses in a business- you must have the intent to make a profit. There are many ways that you can show this including having your own website/Facebook page, showing revenue, having a marketing plan & business plan, and much more.

Alternatively, check out Nineline.com or FreelancePhysician.com for moonlighting opportunities for physicians. You can get paid $150/hour or more. One of my physician friends is now making more money from moonlighting than from his full-time job.

What opportunities could be available to you?

5) Examples of Deductions of Being a Business Owner

Here are some clients who started a business based upon their skills and interests.

Sam and Elizabeth recently retired. When they built their dream home, it was with the longstanding plan that Elizabeth would have an art studio in the home. For years, these plans had taken a backseat to Sam's career while raising the kids.

They added a separate studio, office and classroom. During the week, Elizabeth teaches art, works on commercial graphic design, and creates original paintings to sell at local art fairs. They set up a Limited Liability corporation for the art business.

They were able to write off all costs related to the building and furnishing of the studio and office as well as the prorated share of their home utilities. They used IRS Section 179 of the tax

For more information, go to www.daviddenniston.com/physicians.
For questions, e-mail: dave@daviddenniston.com
Or call 800-548-1820

code to expense up to $125,000 of their tangible personal property expenses for computers, etc., each year.

They write off all materials and business advertising. They write off part of their automotive expenses. Lastly, they write off any other travel-related expenses in selling the art in fairs and exhibits. The write-off allows them to reduce Sam's income tax so their Social Security was not taxed. This led to a reduction of their overall tax percentage.

The art business is beginning to make money. Elizabeth is happy painting and they are living their dream retirement, while saving in income taxes along the way. Because their overall AGI dropped, they were able to write off a greater percentage of their other deductible expenses.

A couple of things to note here:

➢ The business owner doesn't necessarily need to be YOU. It could be a spouse INSTEAD.

➢ There are many potential write-offs including using a home office which allows even more different deductions. Listed below are several deductions worth considering:

- Write off the costs of starting a business
- Use a IRS Section 179 deduction which you can expense tangible, personal property up to $125,000 per year
- Expense travel related to the business
- Take a home office deduction, as well as a part of your utilities
- Write off part of your car if you use it for business
- Buying something you can write for your business that will improve its income prospects while reducing income tax
- Remodel a basement, have a tax deductible home office, and deduct 100 percent of all costs related to the office
- Buy a computer
- Write off some of your insurance costs
- Deduct interest related to the business

2.1 Action Step: What retirement plan do you have (401k/403b/SIMPLE IRA/ etc)? Does it have a match? How much is the match?

How much are you putting in your primary retirement plan annually? Are you maxxing out

For more information, go to www.daviddenniston.com/physician
For questions, e-mail: dave@daviddenniston.co
Or call 800-548-182

your plan? Are you over 50 years old? Are you taking advantage of the catch-up provision?

Write your thoughts down below.

_____

_____

_____

2.2 Action Step: Do you have a second retirement plan (457b)?

How much are you putting in your secondary retirement plan annually? Are you over 50 years old? Are you taking advantage of the catch-up provision?

Write your thoughts down below.

_____

_____

_____

2.3 Action Step: Have you considered setting up your own small business? If you don't have the time, could your spouse start the business instead?

What are your passions? What do you enjoy that could bring in money and give you some great tax deductions?

Make sure to check out FreelancePhysician.com for moonlighting opportunities to make some dough on the side.

Write your thoughts down below.

_____

_____

_____

2.4 Action Step: Do you own your own practice? Are you paid as an independent contractor? Do you have a business on the side?

For more information, go to www.daviddenniston.com/physicians.
For questions, e-mail: dave@daviddenniston.com
Or call 800-548-1820

If you don't have any employees (i.e. a consultant or small business owner), you should strongly consider an Owner Only 401(k) (also called Solo(k) and other similar names).

If you have the ability to sock away _even more money_ or you own your own practice, consider a defined benefit plan or a defined benefit plan with a carve-out. _You can tax deduct tens of thousands of dollars more_ than if you have a traditional 401k/ SIMPLE IRA, etc. These plans are particularly beneficial to owners that are older than their employees or if they only have a few employees who have a short tenure.

Feel free to contact me with any questions about either of those plans. They can be very complex and you want to set them up correctly.

MODULE Three | Managing Capital Gains & Dividends

I have a basic philosophy in life- control the stuff that you can. Understand it, learn about it to empower yourself with the best possible information to make quality decisions.

Unfortunately, we don't have power in many areas in our lives. With the rest, roll with the punches for the stuff that you cannot control. Keep it going and adjust as necessary.

Listen, we can't control what happens in an individual stock or security. Well, maybe Warren Buffet can. I suppose if I had a couple of billion dollars, I could drive up the price of a stock.

Yet, we've all seen people go broke or make really crappy financial decisions.

Here's the thing- you CAN control the capital gains and dividends when you OWN individual stocks and ETFs.

That's because you can sell them AT ANY TIME during the business day. You can sell a position AT A LOSS or AT A GAIN. Nobody is going to force you to sell a position.

Unfortunately, it is much more difficult to control with mutual funds. Let me explain.

For more information, go to www.daviddenniston.com/physicians.
For questions, e-mail: dave@daviddenniston.com
Or call 800-548-1820

<u>Mutual funds can have "phantom capital gains".</u> Essentially, mutual funds will distribute capital gains even when YOU haven't sold anything. Instead, the active manager is buying and selling securities on your behalf. As assets come into the fund, they will buy stocks or other securities. Then, when investors redeem their money, the manager will have to sell stocks or other securities.

This means that are subject to the whim of investors. This can be bad news for tax efficiency! If you are in a "hot fund" that had capital gains from UNSOLD positions that the manager bought years earlier (BEFORE you even invested in the fund) and investors start pulling the dough, you could be left with a BIG tax bill when you don't want it.

As a matter of fact, you could actually LOSE money in a mutual fund and still get caught with a capital gain distribution. Let me explain a case where this happened.

Consider the case of Ivy Global Natural Resources (ticker: IGNYX)...

Performance from 2006 to 2013 (source: Morningstar.com)

2006	2007	2008	2009	2010	2011	2012	2013
+25.98%	+43.72%	-61.27%	+75.14%	+17.19%	-21.39%	+0.49%	+8.19%

Here is the information on capital gains distributions in the same period.

	2006	2007	2008	2009	2010	2011	2012	2013
Price (NAV)			10.31					
ST Cap Gain	0	0	1.3558	0	0	0	0	0
LT Cap Gain	0	0	2.9595	0	0	0	0	0
Gains as %			41.86%					

For more information, go to www.daviddenniston.com/physicians.
For questions, e-mail: dave@daviddenniston.com
Or call 800-548-1820

If you invested on January 1st 2006, you would have been a very happy camper in 2006 and 2007. You would have been up 80% plus in two years! That's awesome.

But, let's say that you held onto the fund through 2008, you would have LOST -61.27% and on top of that because of all the share redemptions, you would have owed taxes- BOTH short-term capital gains (taxed at ordinary income- YUCK) and long-term capital gains (taxed at favorable rates) for a total of 41.86% of your investment!!!

You might be down 30% overall since your initial investment and would have to pay gains on an investment YOU haven't made overall gains on since your initial investment. It's nuts!

However, it could be worse, you could be the poor shmuck who saw the track record in 2006 and 2007 and thought that this investment was a "sure bet" in 2008.

If the poor person, invested $100,000 in IGNYX on 1/1/2008 and didn't sell it by the end of the year, **their investment would have been worth about $39,000 and on TOP of that they would have owed capital gains taxes on about $16,000 of that investment.**

And to add insult to injury, they have NEVER even saw a year of gains in the fund unlike the relatively luckier person who invested on 1/1/2006 who experienced two great years.

Anyhow, needless to say you need to be VERY careful which mutual funds you invest in. Some managers are incredibly tax efficient, but you need to be aware if they are when you are investing non-qualified money.

Now, I'll step off that soap box and we'll focus on more practical ways to help you with "Tax Harvesting".

The basic idea of tax harvesting is that you purposely create CAPITAL GAINS or CAPITAL LOSSES.

Let's go back to the Action Steps in Module 1. Under Action Step 1.2, what showed on line 13 on your form 1040? Was there anything there? Was there a capital gain? A capital loss?

If you had a capital loss, how much did you write-off on your taxes? Did you have a carry-forward capital loss (line 13 of the Schedule D)?

For more information, go to www.daviddenniston.com/physicians.
For questions, e-mail: dave@daviddenniston.com
Or call 800-548-1820

If you had capital gains, here's the rub: the government has NO ceiling on the amount it can tax you. You will get taxed on $3,000 of gain, $25,000 of gain, or even $100,000 of gain if you experience (realized) that gain.

Unfortunately, the reverse is NOT true. The government does have a FLOOR on the losses you can write-off for capital losses. As a matter of fact, you can ONLY write-off $3,000 of losses per year. This is why people have carry-forward losses that rolls over into the following year (or years!). It really ticks me off frankly, but that's the way it is.

What you have to do is MANAGE your capital gains by harvesting what you need.

For example, let's say it is November 30th, you will want to explore your REALIZED and UNREALIZED gains/losses year-to-date.

Perhaps, you have NO carry forward losses and for the year you have realized some capital gains. Review over all of your non-qualified accounts and see if you have a position or two that may have been in the doldrums since you invested.

You may have some CAPITAL LOSSES that you can HARVEST to off-set the gains and even create a loss for the year while continuing to hold onto your winners.

That is tax efficiency, my friends, with you controlling what you can!

By the way, you will want to wait at least 31 days before re-buying that security in order to not get in trouble with the IRS and the SEC. They call this a "wash sale" if you buy it sooner, and that's illegal. Please don't do anything illegal.

Let's flip that scenario around, what if instead you DO have carry forward capital losses? You will instead want to HARVEST your CAPITAL GAINS.

I've seen people with $100,000 or even $200,000 worth of carry-forward losses. At a mere $3,000 year write-off, it would take 33 years to write off $100,000!!

Remember to be careful. It makes good sense to keep $10,000 to $15,000 of losses that you could write-off in the foreseeable future.

Unlike losses, there are no regulations surrounding selling positions at a gain. The IRS doesn't care if you sell it and then buy it back the next year.

> **3.1 Action Step:** Review over your 2008, 2011, and last year's tax returns and Schedule D if you had capital gains or losses. Where did your gains and losses come from? Could your

For more information, go to www.daviddenniston.com/physicians.
For questions, e-mail: dave@daviddenniston.com
Or call 800-548-1820

investments have been managed more tax efficiently?

Have you had any mutual funds with phantom capital gains in 2008 or 2011? Make sure to eliminate the "Ivy Globals" of your portfolio.

Write your thoughts down below.

_____

_____

_____

MODULE

Four

Be Charitable

Some of the best, wonderful things I see clients do is give to others. They give their time, energy, effort and money to some great causes.

Maybe it is to their church or to their alma mater to Big Brothers/Big Sisters or to a local theatre and arts programs. I love seeing clients make an impact in their world!

Beyond your family, what important ways would you like to give back? What causes are you passionate about?

The awesome news is that you can get a tax deduction or even possibly AVOID taxation by unleashing your giving spirit.

In our current tax code, if you are able to get your itemized deductions ABOVE the amount of the standard deduction you can have a higher tax write-off than many Americans.

Keep in mind that your state income taxes are currently counted towards your itemized deductions as well as mortgage interest. By adding some charitable giving to the mix, most of us can easily exceed the standard deduction limits and be able to itemize instead.

For more information, go to www.daviddenniston.com/physicians.
For questions, e-mail: dave@daviddenniston.com
Or call 800-548-1820

What is different from some other itemized deductions is that you don't have to exceed a certain percentage of your income. For example, in order to itemize medical expenses, your medical expenses have to exceed 7.5% of your adjusted gross income, otherwise you cannot itemize them.

In comparison, qualified charitable gifts will deduct substantially from your income if you can itemize. There's no minimum that you must do. Just do something and then do some more and then you will be helping your community and the world as well as getting a tax write-off.

The IRS notes the following on their website. I have bolded and underlined the information that I thought was the most critical:

"To be deductible, charitable contributions must be made to qualified organizations. Payments to individuals are never deductible. See Publication 526, Charitable Contributions. To determine if the organization that you have contributed to qualifies as a charitable organization for income tax deductions, review Exempt Organizations Select Check on the IRS.gov website.

If your contribution entitles you to merchandise, goods, or services, including admission to a charity ball, banquet, theatrical performance, or sporting event, **you can deduct only the amount that exceeds the fair market value of the benefit received.**

For a contribution of cash, check, or other monetary gift (regardless of amount), you must maintain as a record of the contribution a bank record or a written communication from the qualified organization containing the name of the organization, the date of the contribution, and the amount of the contribution. In addition to deducting your cash contributions, you generally can deduct the fair market value of any other property you donate to qualified organizations. See Publication 561, Determining the Value of Donated Property. **For any contribution of $250 or more** (including contributions of cash or property), you must obtain and keep in your records a contemporaneous written acknowledgment from the qualified organization indicating the amount of the cash and a description of any property contributed. The acknowledgment must say whether the organization provided any goods or services in exchange for the gift and, if so, must provide a description and a good faith estimate of the value of those goods or services. One document from the qualified organization may satisfy both the written communication requirement for monetary gifts and the contemporaneous written acknowledgment requirement for all contributions of $250 or more.

You must fill out Form 8283 (PDF), and attach it to your return, if your deduction for a noncash contribution is more than $500. If you claim a deduction for a contribution of noncash property worth $5,000 or less, you must fill out Form 8283, Section A. If you claim a deduction for a

For more information, go to www.daviddenniston.com/physicians.
For questions, e-mail: dave@daviddenniston.com
Or call 800-548-1820

contribution of noncash property worth more than $5,000, you will need a qualified appraisal of the noncash property and must fill out Form 8283, Section B. If you claim a deduction for a contribution of noncash property worth more than $500,000, you also will need to attach the qualified appraisal to your return

Special rules apply to donations of certain types of property such as automobiles, inventory and investments that have appreciated in value. For more information, refer to Publication 526, Charitable Contributions. For information on determining the value of your noncash contributions, refer to Publication 561, Determining the Value of Donated Property."

Here are the main points from this document about charitable giving while getting a tax deduction:

1) Keep great records

2) You can contribute cash or check

3) You can ALSO contribute property or an appreciated asset (but you may need a valuation to be done if it is over $5,000)

I cannot overstate the tremendous implications of having the ability to contribute an appreciate asset. This means that if you have a position with a HUGE unrealized gain, you never have to realize it. Instead, you can gift it (or part of it) to a charitable organization AS IS and receive a deduction for doing so.

There are some other more specialized strategies that many doctors should consider as well.

For example, you can set up your own foundation or charitable remainder trust (CRT) and donate an appreciated asset DIRECTLY to your foundation or CRT and get a tax write-off.

In the case of the foundation, you can distribute a percentage of the foundation to charities of your choice. Essentially, you are maintaining control of an asset and have say over its growth, creating a legacy portfolio that your kids can continue after your passing to continue to make a difference in the world. This is the exact strategy that Bill Gates has employed. This has allowed him to avoid paying hundreds of millions of dollars in capital gains.

Instead, consider the charitable remainder trust. The initial start is the same as a foundation- you can contribute highly appreciated assets and get a tax write-off. Then, you start an income stream back to yourself that is taxable (possibly just partially). Whatever is left in the trust at your passing is contributed to the organizations of your choosing when you established the trust.

For more information, go to www.daviddenniston.com/physicians.
For questions, e-mail: dave@daviddenniston.com
Or call 800-548-1820

Another charitable strategy that I think is far too under-utilized is charitable giving through required minimum distributions.

Once you hit 70.5 years old (don't ask me why the half year, it's the IRS), you HAVE to start taking distributions from your IRA or 401k or 403b (unless you are still working for a given employer).

Many physicians have VERY substantial IRAs. As a matter of fact, I have several clients who are required to take $50,000 to $150,000 in distributions EVERY year. These distributions are normally ENTIRELY taxable.

However, here's the good news- if you instead direct PART or ALL of that to a charitable cause (a qualified entity, not a person). You will NOT have to pay taxes on that part of the distribution.

Again here, by having your own entity like a charitable foundation or CRT, you can have the funds gifted to the places you want, while having control over the investments and allowing them to continue to grow on your own terms over the years.

Make sure to review the tax law before you consider using this loophole. Congress has to approve it every year. As of the time of writing this guide, this is still a strategy that you can employ.

> **4.1 Action Step:** Review over Action Step 1.2 and your last year's tax return. Did you itemize your taxes or take the standard deduction? How close were you to being able to itemize your deductions?
>
> Review over Schedule A in your tax return. What itemized line items were you able to take advantage of?
>
> How much did you give in charitable contributions? Could you do more and take advantage of the tax code?
>
> Write your thoughts down below.
>
> _____
>
> _____
>
> _____

> **4.2 Action Step:** Review over your non-qualified (money that is not in IRA accounts) accounts. Do

31

For more information, go to www.daviddenniston.com/physicians.
For questions, e-mail: dave@daviddenniston.com
Or call 800-548-1820

you have positions with large capital gains?

Do you have need of this money? Could you establish your own foundation or CRT and take the tax write-off?

Are you near or above 70.5 years old? Do you need all of your required minimum distribution? Could you donate some of it?

Write your thoughts down below.

_____

_____

_____

MODULE Five | More Deductions & Write-Offs

Beyond what I have already mentioned, there are a host of regular unreimbursed expenses that many physicians incur annually regardless of whether or not they are a small business owner or own their practice.

You want to make sure to look at each one of these to determine whether or not this may apply to you.

Consider that some physicians are paid via W-2, meaning that they are employees of an organization while other physicians are paid via 1099-MISC, meaning that they are independent contractors.

There are different rules that apply to each.

I've even met and worked with several physicians who are a combination of the two, particularly E.R. doctors who have a seniority status.

MDTaxes.com does a wonderful job of summing up the data in the paragraphs below and in the

For more information, go to www.daviddenniston.com/physicians.
For questions, e-mail: dave@daviddenniston.com
Or call 800-548-1820

accompanying tables.

"How you deduct your allowable unreimbursed professional expenses depends on how you were compensated during the year:

- *Individuals compensated as employees (having taxes withheld from their pay) are required to deduct these type expenses as a miscellaneous itemized deduction on their Schedule A. These individuals are also required to complete and attach a Form 2106 or 2106-EZ, Unreimbursed Employee Business Expense, to their Form 1040.*

- *Individuals compensated as independent contractors (having NO taxes withheld) deduct their professionals' expenses directly against their income. These individuals are required to complete and attach a Schedule C or Schedule C-EZ, Profit or Loss From Business, to their Form 1040.*

- *Individuals compensated as both employees and independent contractors need to determine whether to reflect a specific expense on the Schedule C or the Form 2106. Items which are specifically related to a person's income as an independent contractor, such as malpractice insurance and directly related auto expenses, will be deducted directly against that income. Other items, such as job search expenses, are most likely related to a person's employment and should be reflected on the Form 2106.*

Item	IRS PUB	Deductible	Non-Deductible
Automobile expenses	917	The portion of automobile expenses incurred while driving between two different workplaces, or between your principal residence and a temporary job site. You can base the deduction on actual expenses incurred or on the standard mileage rate.	The portion of automobile expenses incurred while commuting between your principal residence and a regular place of business.
Beepers and pagers	529	The rental fees paid by you for beepers and pagers used in connection with your employment.	Any costs associated with the personal use of these items.
Books/library	534	The cost of reference books purchased during the year. You can also depreciate your "library" the first year you put it into business use, based on the fair market value of the library on that date.	Any books not related to your profession
Cellular phones & internet access	534	The business portion of the cost of the cellular phone can be written off. Plus, you can deduct the business use portion of the monthly cellular phone bills and internet access fees.	Any portion of the cost of the cellular phone and the monthly cellular phone bills and internet access fees relating to personal use.
Computer purchases	534	Depreciation on the business use percent of any computer or peripheral purchased (1) as a requirement of your employment and (2) for the convenience of your	Any computer and peripheral not specifically purchased as a requirement of employment or

For more information, go to www.daviddenniston.com/physicians.
For questions, e-mail: dave@daviddenniston.com
Or call 800-548-1820

		employer.	for the benefit of your employer.
Education, examinations and licenses	508	Expenses incurred that are required as part of your employment and maintain or improve your skills in your current profession.	Expenses incurred that prepare or qualify you for a new trade or business, such as medical or dental school.
Equipment and instruments	534	Depreciation expense on any items purchased during the year, or based on the fair market value of equipment and instruments purchased in previous years but put into business use this year.	Equipment and instruments not associated with your profession.
Home office	587	The percentage of your home (based on square footage) used regularly and exclusively in connection with your profession. Great for renters since rent isn't otherwise deductible on your federal tax return.	The portion of your home used for any non-business purpose during the year, even if just for one day.
Insurance	529	Malpractice insurance and insurance on business assets.	Health, life and disability insurance. Health insurance is deductible as an "adjustment to income" if you have net self-employment income.
Interest on school loans	535	Up to $2,500 of student loan interest paid during the year, subject to income limitations, is deductible as an "adjustment to income". (NOTE: After you have a low to mid-six figure income, school loan interest starts become non-deductible)	Interest on school loans in excess of $2,500 per year.
Job search	529	Expenses associated with finding a new position in your current trade or business.	Any expenses associated with finding your first job, or a job in a new trade or business.
Meals and entertainment	463	50% of the cost of a meal when there is a specific business purpose in connection with the meal, or while temporarily traveling on business.	Personal meals, including meals while on call at a hospital located in the general vicinity of where you live.
Parking and tolls	463	Parking and tolls incurred in connection with traveling between two different workplaces or between your principal residence and a temporary job site.	Parking and tolls incurred in connection with commuting between your principal residence and a regular place of business.
Professional dues, journals and subscriptions	535	Fees paid to join professional organizations or to subscribe to their journals.	Dues paid to social or athletic clubs.
Psychoanalysis	n/a	A licensed psychiatrist or psychologist who is undergoing psychoanalysis as a required part of training in that field.	Any other licensed professional must claim costs associated with

For more information, go to www.daviddenniston.com/physicians.
For questions, e-mail: dave@daviddenniston.com
Or call 800-548-1820

				psychoanalysis as a medical deduction.
Supplies	535	Supplies, such as slides for presentations, that are required in connection with your employment.		Supplies that don't fall within the definition of "ordinary" and "necessary" for a professional in your field.
Temporary job assignments	463	The travel, lodging, and 50% of the cost of the meals incurred during a job rotation outside the general vicinity of where you live. The rotation must be for a specific period of less than one year, and you must intend to return to the city that you were living in prior to the rotation.		Any expense associated with a job rotation outside the general vicinity of where you live that will last for more than a year, or for an unspecified length of time.
Travel and lodging	463	Travel and lodging expenses incurred while outside the general vicinity of your residence in connection with a deductible activity.		Travel and lodging incurred when the primary purpose of the trip is not business related.
Uniforms and cleaning	529	The cost of purchasing and cleaning clothing, such as lab coats and scrubs, required by your employer that isn't considered "everyday street clothing".		Items such as suits, shirts, shoes, ties and wristwatches because they fit the description of "everyday street clothing".

IRS Pub indicates the IRS Publication that contains information on this topic. You can access the IRS Pubs at www.irs.gov.

5.1 Action Step: Review over last year's tax return. What non-reimbursed expenses did you take advantage of? What expenses listed above might you be able to utilize in the future?

Write your thoughts down below.

_____

_____

_____

For more information, go to www.daviddenniston.com/physicians.
For questions, e-mail: dave@daviddenniston.com
Or call 800-548-1820

MODULE	"Back-Door"
Six	Roth IRAs

Way back in the early 2000's, as the Twin Towers toppled in New York, President Bush and a republican congress pushed through temporary tax incentives in order to get businesses to unleash their cash and for consumers and individual investors to have more money in hand to spend in the economy.

Because, these measures were only meant to be temporary, we called this the "sunsetting" of various provisions as they expired in 2010.

Our split congress could NOT agree on what to do in 2010, 2011, or 2012. Capital gains taxes stayed low, estate tax exemption dropped, AND the Roth IRA conversion limit moved from being capped at $100,000 AGI to being UNLIMITED.

Our crazy congress went right to the brink, flirting with the idea of going into default on our debts. Essentially, the government was playing a game of chicken, seeing who would swerve off the road first.

Finally, at the very very end of 2012, our government was done playing games (for now?) and came to a settlement. The result was that there were a number of provisions that changed with the fiscal cliff.

However, there are quite a few that have not, including Roth IRA conversions.

The purpose of this module is to do a quick overview of traditional IRA versus Roth IRA and *then let you in on the secret of*, <u>if you are still working, how you could put money into a Roth IRA regardless of what your income tax bracket is.</u>

Then finally, we'll address some of the pitfalls and caveats of doing a Roth IRA conversion.

First, why put money in a traditional IRA or a Roth IRA?

It's all about trying to be as tax efficient as possible and keep money out of Uncle Sam's hands whether in the short-term or long-term.

Traditional IRAs, 401ks, and 403bs are all focused on trying to do one thing- save money on taxes today! In the case of the traditional IRA, if you fall within given tax situation and you are currently having income that you earn from a job, you can make a contribution and every last cent is tax deductible and you can write off the contribution on your taxes.

However, by getting a tax deduction today, you are waiting to pay federal/state income taxes on those funds until you withdraw that money.

For more information, go to www.daviddenniston.com/physicians
For questions, e-mail: dave@daviddenniston.com
Or call 800-548-1820

Here's where your income would need to be in order for this to happen:

IRA Deduction if You ARE Covered by a Retirement Plan at Work - 2013

If Your Filing Status Is...	And Your Modified AGI Is...	Then You Can Take...
single or **head of household**	$59,000 or less	$5,500 if under 50, $6,500 if over 50
	more than $59,000 but less than $69,000	a partial deduction.
	$69,000 or more	no deduction.
married filing jointly or **qualifying widow(er)**	$95,000 or less	$5,500 if under 50, $6,500 if over 50
	more than $95,000 but less than $115,000	a partial deduction.
	$115,000 or more	no deduction.
married filing separately	less than $10,000	a partial deduction.
	$10,000 or more	no deduction.

Source: http://www.irs.gov/Retirement-Plans/2013-IRA-Deduction-Limits-Effect-of-Modified-AGI-on-Deduction-if-You-Are-Covered-by-a-Retirement-Plan-at-Work

Meanwhile, Roth IRAs are focused on saving money on taxes later.

The basic concept is that you have already paid taxes on the money and so when you withdraw the money after being 60 years old, you don't have to pay any taxes on the money you put in or its growth!

Under normal circumstances, here's where your income would need to be in order to contribute to a Roth:

Roth IRA Contributions in 2013

If your filing status is...	And your modified AGI is...	Then you can contribute...
married filing jointly or **qualifying widow(er)**	< $178,000	$5,500 if under 50, $6,500 if over 50
	≥ $178,000 but < $188,000	a reduced amount
	≥ $188,000	Zero
married filing separately and you lived with your spouse at any time during the year	< $10,000	a reduced amount
	≥ $10,000	Zero
single, **head of household**, or	< $112,000	$5,500 if under 50,

For more information, go to www.daviddenniston.com/physicians.
For questions, e-mail: dave@daviddenniston.com
Or call 800-548-1820

married filing separately and you did not live with your spouse at any time during the year		$6,500 if over 50
	> $112,000 but < $127,000	a reduced amount
	> $127,000	Zero

Source: http://www.irs.gov/Retirement-Plans/Amount-of-Roth-IRA-Contributions-That-You-Can-Make-For-2013

However, this is where things start to get interesting.

What if your AGI is over 188k? You'd look at this table and think, man, I can't make an IRA contribution or a Roth IRA contribution!

Guess what? Like many other things with the government, there's certain caveats to be aware of.

What you can do is contribute to a non-deductible IRA where you don't get a tax deduction and no income restriction for putting money in, but then no matter your income, you can convert those funds from the non-deductible IRA to a Roth IRA.

Back in 2010 when a bunch of tax incentives began to sunset, part of the package was to lift the cap off of Roth IRA conversions. Prior to 2010, if you were married and your income was over 100k, you couldn't convert to a Roth. However, since then, there is no income restriction!

They have continued this provision in 2011, 2012, 2013, and now 2014.

The bottom line here is through a bit of paperwork shuffling and moving assets around, no matter your income, you have the ability to contribute to a Roth.

It's crazy! I don't know why they don't just lift the income cap off of the Roth IRA. I guess that's the insanity of government for you.

This is a fantastic financial planning tool, but I do want to point out a couple of pointers and pitfalls.

First, make sure that your non-deductible IRA contribution is set up in a completely separate account from any deductible IRA money. If you mix the two together, it can become a paperwork nightmare to track.

Secondly, the best possible scenario for a straight-forward conversion is to have no traditional tax-deductible IRA money at all for example in in 401ks, 403bs, and 457 DC. However, if you have traditional tax-deductible IRA funds, you have to convert pro-rata that money into the Roth as well and it becomes a taxable transaction.

Disclaimer: It may not be beneficial to convert in all cases, particular when there is taxable money involved. You're essentially betting that your tax rate will be higher in retirement than it is now. You are choosing to pay that cost now rather than later. Note that it may take 5 years or longer to have this be beneficial.

For more information, go to www.daviddenniston.com/physicians.
For questions, e-mail: dave@daviddenniston.com
Or call 800-548-1820

Third, you want to IMMEDIATELY convert (assuming no tax consequences from other IRA money) to a Roth IRA. You DO NOT want to have earnings on the non-deductible IRA. This could lead to additional taxes when you do convert.

Fourth, SPOUSES can be treated differently. If one spouse has a significant amount of traditional tax deductible IRA money and the other spouse has NO tax-deductible IRA money. Use the "other spouse" to contribute to a non-deductible IRA then contribute to the Roth. **YOU WANT TO AVOID utilizing the spouse WITH IRA money WHEN YOU HAVE A CHOICE.**

Let me show you two examples (for illustrative purposes only):

Example One: John has $100,000 in traditional tax-deductible IRA, $100,000 in his 401k, and $5,000 he contributed to a non-deductible IRA. If he wanted to convert the $5,000 non-deductible to a Roth IRA, he could only move over part of it as non-taxable. The majority would be taxed. How do you figure this out?

You ignore the 100k in 401k money, it doesn't count. You add up the 100k in tax-deductible IRA + the 5k in non-deductible IRA which gives us a total of 105k. 5k divided by 105k gives us 4.8%. So, more than 95% of this conversion would be taxed. Of the 5k non-deductible, he'd only move about $250 to a Roth IRA.

Not a great situation- John probably wouldn't want to go through the hassle of this process.

Example Two: John has $2,000 in traditional tax-deductible IRA, $100,000 in his 401k, and $5,000 he contributed to a non-deductible IRA. If he wanted to convert the $5,000 non-deductible to a Roth IRA, he could do almost all of it as non-taxable and then next year, assuming the same rules apply, do even more.

Once again you ignore the 100k in 401k money, it doesn't count. You add up the 2k in tax-deductible IRA + the 5k in non-deductible IRA which gives us a total of 7k. 5k divided by 7k gives us 71.4%. So, less than 30% of this conversion would be taxed. Of the 5k non-deductible, he'd move about $3.5k to a Roth IRA without it being taxed. He'd also move 1.5k of the tax-deductible to a Roth IRA, which would be taxed.

Of course, the best situation is having no tax-deductible IRA money, because then you can convert 100%. However, given the example we showed above, within a couple of years, a relatively small old IRA account could work as well as it whittles down to virtually nothing!

Note that this is done on an individual basis. For married spouses, you could have one spouse with a bunch of deductible IRA money and the other with none. You could do the tax-free conversion focusing on the spouse that has no deductible IRA money!

Lastly, make sure you are filing the right tax forms when going through this process. For doing the Roth IRA conversion, you will receive a form 1099 from your brokerage company. This will say that it is a

For more information, go to www.daviddenniston.com/physicians.
For questions, e-mail: dave@daviddenniston.com
Or call 800-548-1820

taxable transaction. In order to get this corrected, you'll want to file the form 8606 for nondeductible IRAs which tracks the calculations we described in our previous examples.

You can see how to do this on TurboTax by going to the following link:

http://thefinancebuff.com/how-to-report-backdoor-roth-in-turbotax.html

Let me brief describe to you what you'll want to check off (assuming you are OUT of the tax bracket to get a deduction):

1) List and confirm that you contributed to a Traditional IRA

2) You did NOT switch or recharacterize the contribution.

3) You made AND tracked non-deductible contributions to your IRA

4) Your IRA deduction should be ZERO

5) You should have received a 1099R form from your broker/clearing firm

6) IMPORTANT: Your 1099 may show a taxable distribution AND taxable amount of same amount BUT the taxable amount NOT determined should be checked off

7) You then note that you moved the money to another retirement account & CONVERTED the money to a Roth IRA

8) YOUR DOUBLE CHECK IS LINE 15B WHICH SHOULD BE ZERO IF YOU IMMEDIATELY CONVERTED WITH NO EARNINGS

6.1 Action Step: Below, list what you have in 401(k)'s, 403(b)'s, 457 DC, Traditional IRA, and Roth IRAs for yourself and your spouse...

	401(k) Value	403(b) Value	457 DC Value	Traditional IRA Value	NonDeductible IRA Value	Roth IRA Value
Spouse#1						
Spouse# 2						

For more information, go to www.daviddenniston.com/physicians.
For questions, e-mail: dave@daviddenniston.com
Or call 800-548-1820

6.2 Action Step: Review over the table above. Do either you or your spouse have money in traditional tax-deductible IRA? IF MAKING THE BACK-DOOR ROTH- MAKE SURE TO USE THE SPOUSE with the LEAST AMOUNT of Traditional tax-deductible IRA.

<u>REMEMBER- the amount in 401ks, 457 DC, and 403(b) DOES NOT COUNT in the Roth Conversion.</u>

Consider moving the traditional tax-deductible IRA to your current employer sponsored plan so that NEXT year you could take full advantage of the back-door Roth.

Write down your thoughts below.

_____

_____

_____

Disclaimer: Please note that this should not be taken as specific investment or tax advice and you should consult a professional before deciding whether a conversion may be right for you.

For more information, go to www.daviddenniston.com/physicians.
For questions, e-mail: dave@daviddenniston.com
Or call 800-548-1820

Final Thoughts

Congratulations! You've just accomplished something that very few people have every done in their lives.

You have taken the time to invest into your future. You have learning about taxes and how to be proactive. You've learned about the most important deductions that you can take advantage of in order to minimize taxes.

Just as importantly, you've gone through some action steps with specific follow-ups that you can apply immediately!

Take the next step- implement those promises you made to yourself.

We cannot control so many things in our lives- the weather, your favorite sports team winning the big game, being sick, a family member passing away, children that make poor decisions, and so much more.

However, your taxes and how you treat them **are in your power**. Take control today. Be proactive. You can do it!

I encourage you to revisit this workbook on an annual basis. I will make updates based on your feedback. So, please let me know your experience and where I can improve.

If you would like any additional support and to learn more about how I can serve you, please feel free to contact me anytime at dave@daviddenniston.com or call me at (800) 548-1890.

Let's take this journey together and get you on the path to financial freedom.

Warm Regards,

Dave Denniston

For more information, go to www.daviddenniston.com/physicians.
For questions, e-mail: dave@daviddenniston.com
Or call 800-548-182C

Made in the USA
Coppell, TX
01 March 2024

29604408R00024